I0820606

Designed by Nature

Everyday Inventions

Samantha S. Bell
and John Willis

MEDIA ENHANCED BOOKS
AV2 BY WEIGL
ADDED VALUE • AUDIO VISUAL
www.av2books.com

Go to www.av2books.com, and enter this book's unique code.

BOOK CODE

AVQ84366

AV² by Weigl brings you media enhanced books that support active learning.

AV² provides enriched content that supplements and complements this book. Weigl's AV² books strive to create inspired learning and engage young minds in a total learning experience.

Your AV² Media Enhanced books come alive with...

Audio
Listen to sections of the book read aloud.

Key Words
Study vocabulary, and complete a matching word activity.

Video
Watch informative video clips.

Quizzes
Test your knowledge.

Embedded Weblinks
Gain additional information for research.

Slide Show
View images and captions, and prepare a presentation.

Try This!
Complete activities and hands-on experiments.

... and much, much more!

Published by AV² by Weigl
350 5th Avenue, 59th Floor
New York, NY 10118
Website: www.av2books.com

Library of Congress Cataloging-in-Publication Data available upon request.
Fax 1-866-44-WEIGL for the attention of the Publishing Records department.

ISBN 978-1-4896-9717-2 (hardcover)
ISBN 978-1-4896-9718-9 (softcover)
ISBN 978-1-4896-9719-6 (multi-user eBook)
ISBN 978-1-4896-9720-2 (single-user eBook)

Printed in the United States of America in Brainerd, Minnesota
1 2 3 4 5 6 7 8 9 0 22 21 20 19 18

122018
102318

Project Coordinator: John Willis   Designer: Ana María Vidal

Every reasonable effort has been made to trace ownership and to obtain permission to reprint copyright material. The publishers would be pleased to have any errors or omissions brought to their attention so that they may be corrected in subsequent printings.

Weigl acknowledges Alamy, Getty Images, iStock, Minden Pictures, and Shutterstock as its primary image suppliers for this title.

First published by North Star Editions in 2019

Designed by Nature

Contents

Chapter 1

Scientists of biomimicry study plants and animals in their labs.

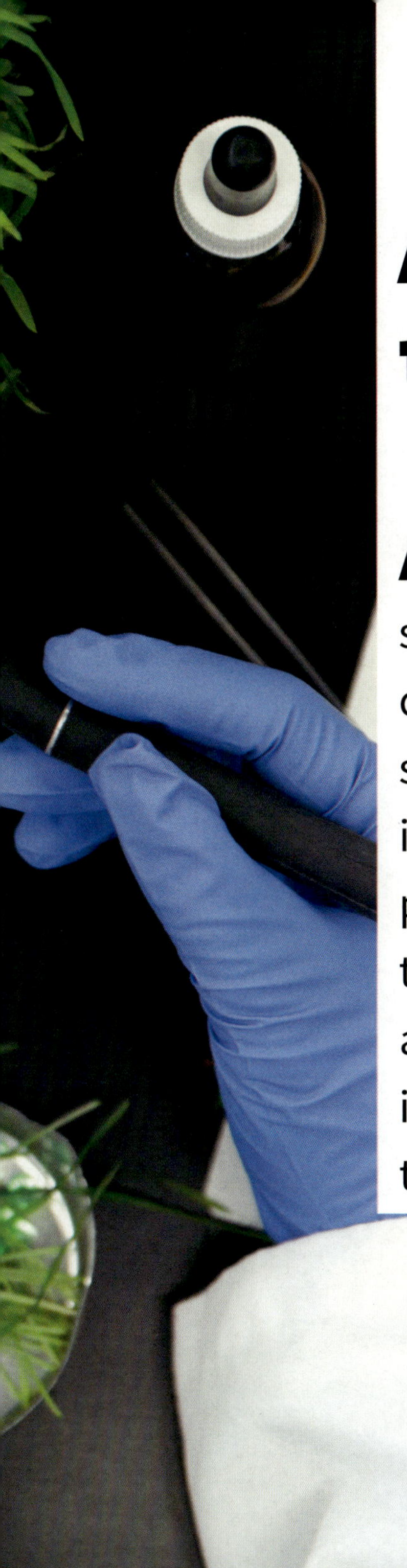

Around the House

An invention is a new product, process, or way of doing something. Many inventions make certain jobs easier to do. Others help solve specific problems. One way inventors and scientists are solving problems is through biomimicry. In this process, scientists use nature as a guide. First, they observe patterns in nature. Then, they create designs that are similar to nature's designs.

A cat's paw
widens when its claws
are extended.

Nature has inspired many everyday objects around the house. For example, in 2011, one inventor studied cats' claws to create a safer thumbtack. Regular tacks have sharp pins. They are easy to drop on the floor, where people can step on them.

The pins on the new tacks can be drawn in, similar to the way a cat retracts its claws. In this design, a **sheath** covers the pin. The sheath is made of a rubberlike plastic. The pin stays tucked inside the sheath until pressed into a hard surface.

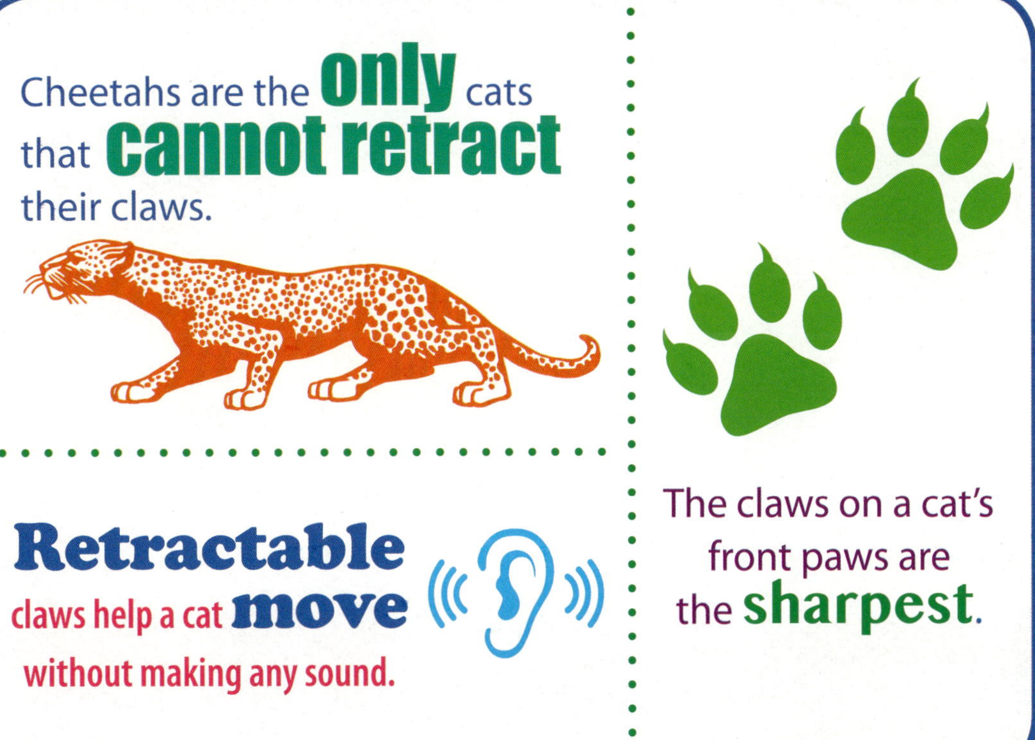

Sticking with Geckos

Geckos can cling to wet surfaces. They crawl on wet leaves and branches in their rainy habitats. However, geckos stick best to surfaces that are not completely wet. Their toes create air pockets that keep their feet dry. Scientists hope to make waterproof **adhesives** based on gecko toes.

Other scientists studied the feet of geckos. These small lizards can climb up walls. Geckos have stiff **tendons** on their toe pads. These tendons help the gecko grip surfaces. Geckos' toe pads also have millions of tiny hairs. To climb, the gecko places its toe pad on a surface. When it pulls the toe back, the hairs stick to the surface. The hairs unstick when the gecko pulls in a different direction.

Most adhesives are gooey or soft. In 2012, geckos gave scientists a new idea. The scientists created a stiff adhesive. The adhesive is so strong that one small piece can hold up to 700 pounds (318 kilograms). But it can still be removed easily. The material peels off when pulled upward.

Thanks to cats and geckos, thumbtacks and adhesives are safer and easier to use. Plants and animals are nature's engineers. They are able to **adapt** and thrive on Earth. They do not harm their environments with waste or pollution. Many scientists believe inventions should work more like the natural world.

The hairs on a gecko's feet are known as setae.

Chapter 2

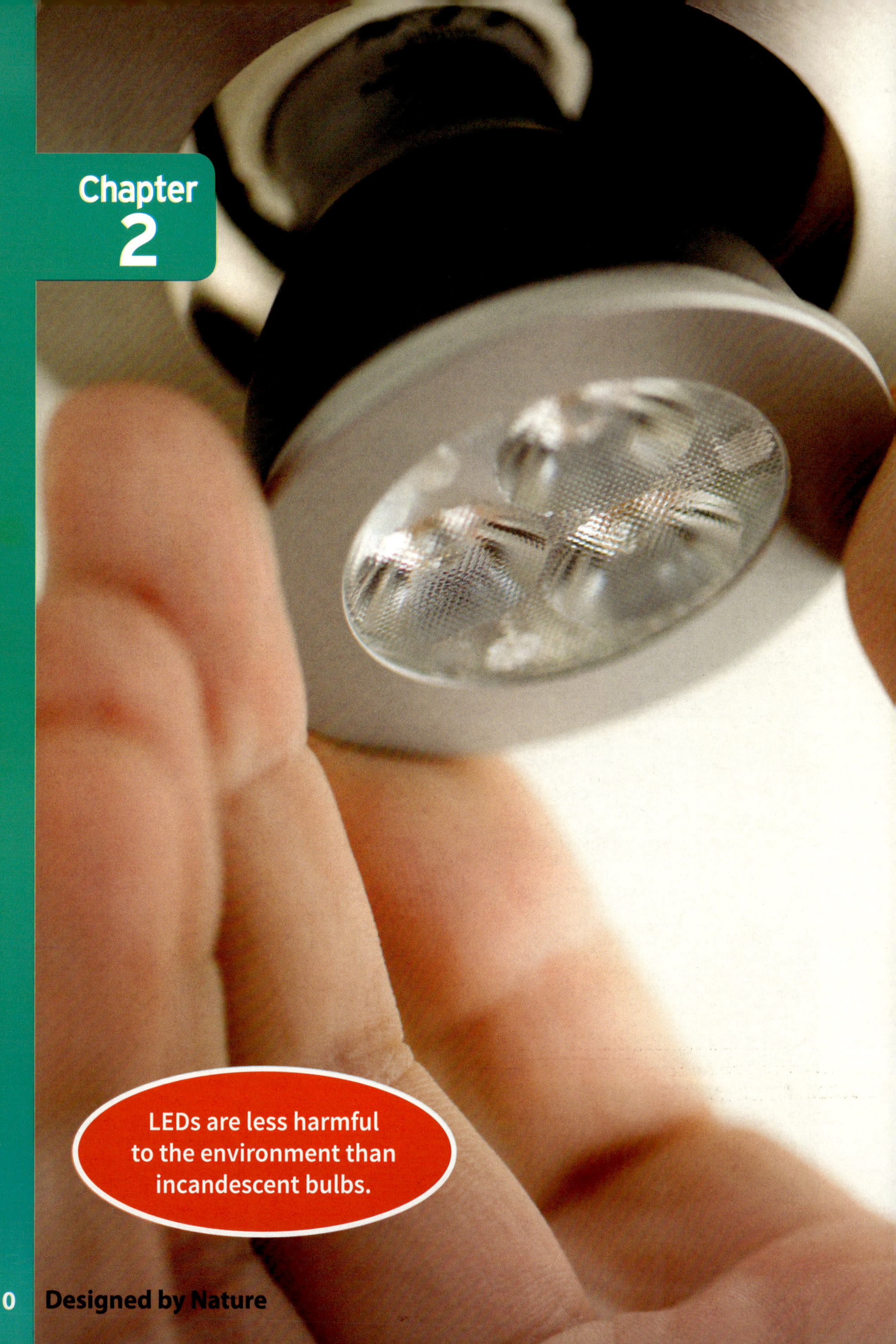

LEDs are less harmful to the environment than incandescent bulbs.

High-Tech Improvements

Some nature-inspired inventions improve other machines or products. These are called innovations. For example, many people no longer use **incandescent** light bulbs. Instead, they use LEDs, or light-emitting diodes. These light bulbs use less energy than older bulbs. They also last much longer.

The first LED light bulbs did not give off enough light. Some of the light was trapped inside the bulbs. Scientists looked to fireflies for an answer. They studied the firefly's light organ. This part of the firefly's body gives off light.

The scientists discovered that the light organ is covered in scales. They also found that the scales do not fit together. Instead, the scales look like shingles on a roof. The sharp edges of the scales cause light rays to scatter. This makes the light look brighter. In 2013, scientists added a similar surface to LED light bulbs. The new surface made the light bulbs 55 percent brighter.

Fireflies glow because of a chemical reaction in their light organs.

Scientists also studied the morpho butterfly's wings. Morpho wings have tiny plates that reflect light. Ridges on the plates form specific patterns. They give the wings a shimmery blue color. In 2009, scientists used a similar design to create a new e-reader. Other e-readers create their own light. But the new e-reader reflects the light around it.

New solar panels can absorb light even as the Sun sets.

The e-reader has tiny mirrors under its screen. The mirrors move in **microseconds**. Similar to morpho wings, the mirrors make patterns to create color images. Reflecting light uses less energy than creating new light. It also makes the screen easier to see in bright light.

Butterflies have also inspired other inventions. One species, called the common rose butterfly, has black wings. Its wings have scales with tiny holes. The holes scatter the sunlight that hits them. That way, the wings can absorb more of the Sun's heat. The holes also make the wings lighter. In 2017, scientists used a similar method to help solar panels absorb more light. They created panels with tiny holes. Usually, solar panels must be pointed directly at the Sun. But the tiny holes could catch light at an angle. This allowed the panels to absorb more light during daylight hours. As a result, they produced more power. The holes also made the panels lighter.

Chapter 3

Insects may be attracted to the ultraviolet light reflected by spiderwebs.

Better Buildings

Nature could be the key to improving the designs of buildings. For example, the orb-weaver spider spins a complex web. The spider's silk reflects **ultraviolet** light. As a result, birds can see the web. They do not fly into it. In 2006, scientists created a coating that works similarly to a spiderweb. It reflects ultraviolet light.

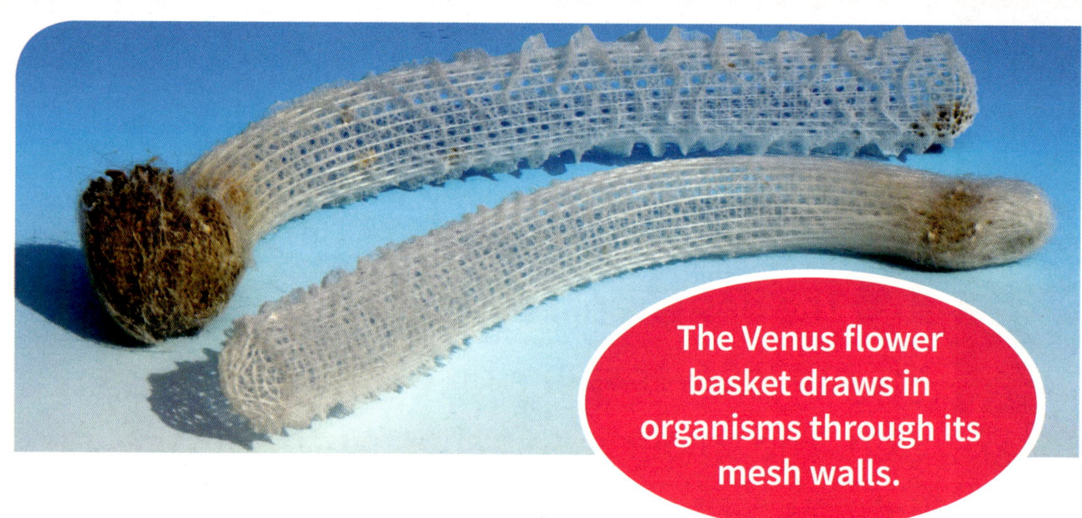

The Venus flower basket draws in organisms through its mesh walls.

The coating makes windows more visible to birds. That way, the birds do not fly into them. Fewer birds are hurt or killed.

Plants have also helped improve buildings. The lotus plant grows in muddy water. But the plant never looks dirty. It has waxy, waterproof leaves and flowers. These leaves are covered in tiny bumps and hairs. When it rains, the small bumps help the rain wash dirt off the plant.

In 2005, scientists came up with a lotus-inspired design for self-cleaning paint. The paint creates a bumpy surface on the wall of the building, similar to the lotus flower. When it rains, the water pushes away dirt, keeping the wall clean.

Some buildings even get their shape from nature. The Gherkin is a tower in London, England. It was completed in 2003. The Gherkin's architects were inspired by the Venus flower basket. This tube-shaped sea sponge has a **lattice**-like structure. The mesh pattern makes the sponge very strong.

Designed by Nature

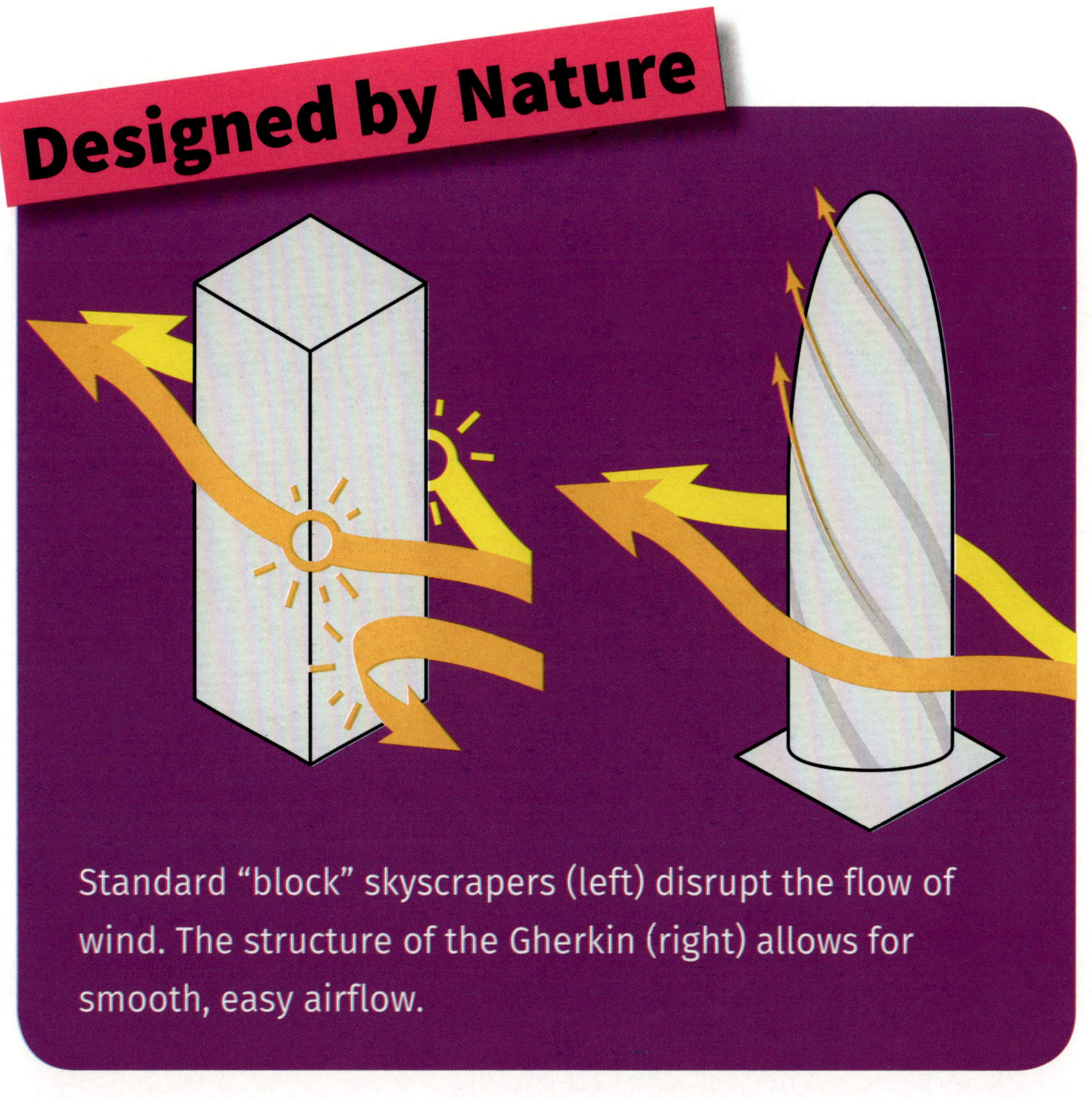

Standard "block" skyscrapers (left) disrupt the flow of wind. The structure of the Gherkin (right) allows for smooth, easy airflow.

The Gherkin's outer walls use a similar pattern. This design helps make the building strong. It also creates a natural **ventilation** system. The tower's curved walls allow more air to flow faster around it. Large vents at the bottom suck in the air and move it upward. This helps the building stay cool, requiring less air conditioning.

Keeping Cool

Termite mounds maintain a constant temperature. Their shape helps with this process. Cool air comes in at the base of the mound. It moves upward into the mound's warmer areas. Scientists designed a similar system for the Eastgate Centre. This shopping center and office complex is in Harare, Zimbabwe. It uses only one-tenth of the energy needed to cool other buildings of the same size.

Inspire Me!

Echolocation

Many people who are blind use a cane to get around. One scientist is studying bats to make a new type of cane. Bats use a process called echolocation to navigate in the dark. As a bat flies, it makes sounds through its mouth and nose. When the sound waves hit objects, they create echoes. The bat uses the echoes to create a map of its surroundings.

The new cane will work in a similar way. The cane sends out **ultrasonic** waves. Some of the sound waves will sense large, stationary objects. Other sound waves will sense smaller, fast-moving objects. The waves hit an object and bounce back. Then the cane vibrates. The vibrations tell the person where the objects are.

People who are blind use probing canes to sense objects.

Chapter 4

Building construction makes up 30 percent of energy use in the United States.

For the Future

Scientists and inventors continue to find new ideas. For example, engineers are creating new types of materials for buildings. Today, most buildings are made of concrete and steel. These materials must be made at a very high temperature and pressure. This takes a lot of energy. It also produces carbon dioxide emissions. An emission is a release of gas into the space around Earth. High carbon dioxide emissions are harmful to the planet.

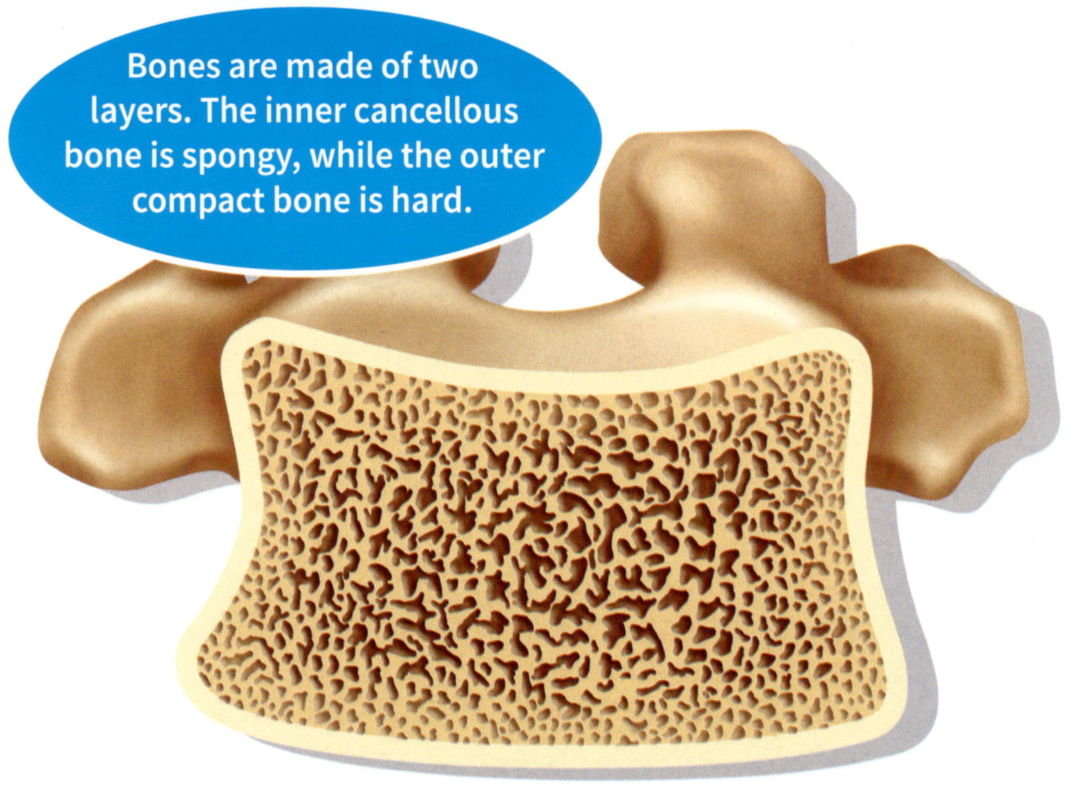

New types of building materials could be better for Earth. One engineer is studying bones and eggshells. Bones are made from minerals and proteins. Minerals make the bones stiff and hard. Proteins make them strong. Eggshells are also made of minerals. Even though eggshells are very thin, they are strong. The engineer created small samples of artificial bone and eggshells. She made the samples at room temperature. They did not take much energy to produce. One day, these materials could be used to construct buildings.

A company called Encycle is working on a nature-inspired home improvement. Scientists at the company studied the way bees communicate. In a swarm of bees, each bee helps the entire colony. But the bees don't need instruction from the queen bee. They automatically work together.

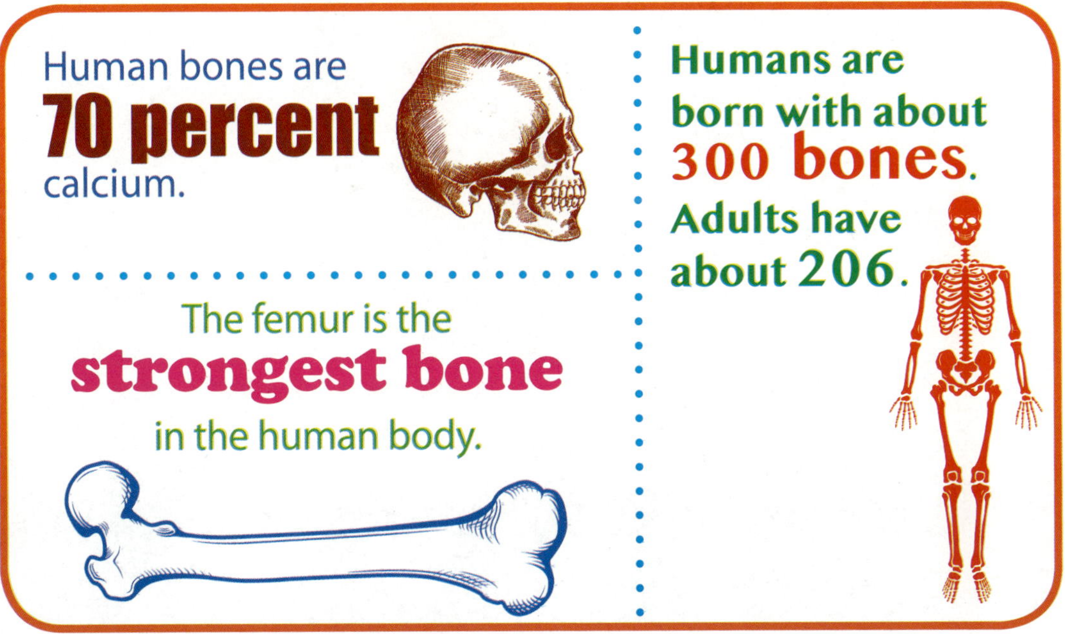

Scientists are using this information to help manage energy in homes. Home appliances usually work independently. The new energy system allows appliances to share information. This way, they can spread out the demand for energy. Each appliance turns on and off based on the demand of the other appliances. This could lower buildings' electric bills.

These inventions are not yet finished. But they could have long-lasting effects. By looking to nature, scientists find new answers to old problems. Their inventions can make everyday life easier and safer.

Timeline

Humans have been using nature to develop everyday technology for many years. As people understand more about nature, they are able to make designs more efficient and effective.

1941 Inventor George de Mestral, inspired by burrs, creates Velcro fasteners.

1994 British Telecom, a phone company, uses the behavior of an ant colony to make their computer systems more adaptable.

2011 American engineer Toshi Fukaya invents a cat-claw-based thumbtack. It wins the 2011 Red Dot Award for Design Concept.

2012 A start-up company in the United States begins work on a self-filling water bottle based on the shell of Namib Desert beetles.

2013 Felsuma is founded. This company develops and sells adhesive products based on gecko feet.

2017 Researchers at Germany's Karlsruhe Institute of Technology use the structure of common rose butterfly wings to make solar panels more efficient.

Everyday Inventions Map

Atlantic Ocean

South America

People use many kinds of technology every day. Today, companies and organizations around the world are turning to nature to inspire more efficient and effective designs.

Legend
Water
Land
Scale 0 2,000 Miles 2,000 Kilometers

United States

Every year, the Biomimicry Institute in Missoula, Montana, hosts a design challenge. Teams look to nature to solve a global problem. The Institute hopes the challenge will lead to more nature-inspired inventions.

Great Britain

In 2015, researchers at University College London developed a self-cleaning paint. Based on plants such as lotuses and taro, it causes water droplets on its surface to act as miniature vacuums, cleaning it.

Germany

Arnold Glas, a company headquartered in Remshalden, Germany, developed bird-friendly glass that is now sold and used in offices around the world. The glass reduces bird strikes by about 75 percent.

Australia

Baleen Filters Pty Limited is based out of Adelaide, Australia. Inspired by the baleen found in the mouths of whales, this company produces self-cleaning water filters.

Quiz

1 What is reflected by orb-weaver spider silk?

Answer: Ultraviolet light

2 Where is Arnold Glas headquartered?

Answer: Remshalden, Germany

3 What is the strongest bone in the human body?

Answer: The femur

4 Which butterfly has tiny, light-scattering holes in its wings?

Answer: The rose butterfly

5 What are setae?

Answer: The hairs on a gecko's feet

6 What happens to a cat's paw when it extends its claws?

Answer: It widens

7 What do bats use to map their surroundings?

Answer: Echolocation

8 How many layers are bones made of?

Answer: Two

9 How much energy use in American homes goes toward appliances, electronics, and lighting?

Answer: Nearly 35 percent

10 Are LEDs more harmful to the environment than incandescent bulbs?

Answer: No

Key Words

adapt: to change over time to deal with a certain situation

adhesives: substances used for sticking objects together

incandescent: a type of light bulb that gives off light when heated

lattice: a structure made of strips that cross one another

microseconds: units that are one-millionth of a second

sheath: a close-fitting cover, often for something sharp

tendons: tissues in the body that attach muscles to bones

ultrasonic: having to do with sounds that are too high for humans to hear

ultraviolet: light that is invisible to human eyes and has a shorter wavelength than that of visible light

ventilation: the process of allowing fresh air to enter and move through a room or building

Index

Log on to www.av2books.com

AV² by Weigl brings you media enhanced books that support active learning. Go to www.av2books.com, and enter the special code found on page 2 of this book. You will gain access to enriched and enhanced content that supplements and complements this book. Content includes video, audio, weblinks, quizzes, a slide show, and activities.

AV² Online Navigation

Audio
Listen to sections of the book read aloud.

Book Pages
AV² pages directly correspond to pages in the book.

Video
Watch informative video clips.

Embedded Weblinks
Gain additional information for research.

Key Words
Study vocabulary, and complete a matching word activity.

Try This!
Complete activities and hands-on experiments.

Quizzes
Test your knowledge.

Slide Show
View images and captions, and prepare a presentation.

AV² was built to bridge the gap between print and digital. We encourage you to tell us what you like and what you want to see in the future.

Sign up to be an AV² Ambassador at www.av2books.com/ambassador.

Due to the dynamic nature of the Internet, some of the URLs and activities provided as part of AV² by Weigl may have changed or ceased to exist. AV² by Weigl accepts no responsibility for any such changes. All media enhanced books are regularly monitored to update addresses and sites in a timely manner. Contact AV² by Weigl at 1-866-649-3445 or av2books@weigl.com with any questions, comments, or feedback.